CAMBRIDGE LIBRARY COLLECTION

Books of enduring scholarly value

Religion

For centuries, scripture and theology were the focus of prodigious amounts of scholarship and publishing, dominated in the English-speaking world by the work of Protestant Christians. Enlightenment philosophy and science, anthropology, ethnology and the colonial experience all brought new perspectives, lively debates and heated controversies to the study of religion and its role in the world, many of which continue to this day. This series explores the editing and interpretation of religious texts, the history of religious ideas and institutions, and not least the encounter between religion and science.

Shinto

The diplomat and Japanese and Korean scholar William George Aston (1841–1911) wrote several highly regarded publications, particularly on the Japanese language. Condensed from his more comprehensive 1905 study of the subject, this 1907 work is a brief introduction to Shinto, the indigenous religion of Japan. Based on the worship of nature and ancestor spirits, Shinto has evolved throughout its history, particularly under Buddhist and Confucian influence. In the late nineteenth century it played a notable role in the revival of Japanese nationalism, and continued to be central to public life until 1945. This work focuses on describing its general character, and its myths and practices, drawing on early written sources based on the oral tradition. Aston's work has been criticised for its dependence on philological study of the early texts, but his expertise is undeniable. His groundbreaking *History of Japanese Literature* (1899) is also reissued in this series.

Cambridge University Press has long been a pioneer in the reissuing of out-of-print titles from its own backlist, producing digital reprints of books that are still sought after by scholars and students but could not be reprinted economically using traditional technology. The Cambridge Library Collection extends this activity to a wider range of books which are still of importance to researchers and professionals, either for the source material they contain, or as landmarks in the history of their academic discipline.

Drawing from the world-renowned collections in the Cambridge University Library and other partner libraries, and guided by the advice of experts in each subject area, Cambridge University Press is using state-of-the-art scanning machines in its own Printing House to capture the content of each book selected for inclusion. The files are processed to give a consistently clear, crisp image, and the books finished to the high quality standard for which the Press is recognised around the world. The latest print-on-demand technology ensures that the books will remain available indefinitely, and that orders for single or multiple copies can quickly be supplied.

The Cambridge Library Collection brings back to life books of enduring scholarly value (including out-of-copyright works originally issued by other publishers) across a wide range of disciplines in the humanities and social sciences and in science and technology.

Shinto

The Ancient Religion of Japan

W.G. ASTON

CAMBRIDGE
UNIVERSITY PRESS

CAMBRIDGE
UNIVERSITY PRESS

University Printing House, Cambridge, CB2 8BS, United Kingdom

Cambridge University Press is part of the University of Cambridge.
It furthers the University's mission by disseminating knowledge in the pursuit of
education, learning and research at the highest international levels of excellence.

www.cambridge.org
Information on this title: www.cambridge.org/9781108080927

© in this compilation Cambridge University Press 2015

This edition first published 1907
This digitally printed version 2015

ISBN 978-1-108-08092-7 Paperback

This book reproduces the text of the original edition. The content and language reflect
the beliefs, practices and terminology of their time, and have not been updated.

Cambridge University Press wishes to make clear that the book, unless originally published
by Cambridge, is not being republished by, in association or collaboration with,
or with the endorsement or approval of, the original publisher or its successors in title.

Religions Ancient and Modern

SHINTO: THE ANCIENT
RELIGION OF JAPAN

RELIGIONS: ANCIENT AND MODERN.

Foolscap 8vo. Price 1s. net per Volume.

ANIMISM.
By EDWARD CLODD, Author of *The Story of Creation.*

PANTHEISM.
By JAMES ALLANSON PICTON, Author of *The Religion of the Universe.*

THE RELIGIONS OF ANCIENT CHINA.
By Professor GILES, LL.D., Professor of Chinese in the University of Cambridge.

THE RELIGION OF ANCIENT GREECE.
By JANE HARRISON, Lecturer at Newnham College, Cambridge, Author of *Prolegomena to Study of Greek Religion.*

ISLAM.
By SYED AMEER ALI, M.A., C.I.E., late of H.M.'s High Court of Judicature in Bengal, Author of *The Spirit of Islam* and *The Ethics of Islam.*

MAGIC AND FETISHISM.
By Dr. A. C. HADDON, F.R.S., Lecturer on Ethnology at Cambridge University.

THE RELIGION OF ANCIENT EGYPT.
By Professor W. M. FLINDERS PETRIE, F.R.S.

THE RELIGION OF BABYLONIA AND ASSYRIA.
By THEOPHILUS G. PINCHES, late of the British Museum.

HINDUISM.
By Dr. L. D. BARNETT, of the Department of Oriental Printed Books and MSS., British Museum.

SCANDINAVIAN RELIGION.
By WILLIAM A. CRAIGIE, Joint Editor of the *Oxford English Dictionary.*

CELTIC RELIGION.
By Professor ANWYL, Professor of Welsh at University College, Aberystwyth.

THE MYTHOLOGY OF ANCIENT BRITAIN AND IRELAND.
By CHARLES SQUIRE, Author of *The Mythology of the British Islands.*

JUDAISM.
By ISRAEL ABRAHAMS, M.A., Reader in Talmudic Literature in Cambridge University, Author of *Jewish Life in the Middle Ages.*

SHINTO: THE RELIGION OF OLD JAPAN.
By W. G. ASTON, C.M.G., Author of *A History of Japanese Literature.* [*Nearly Ready.*

ISLAM IN INDIA.
By T. W. ARNOLD, Assistant Librarian at the India Office, Author of *The Preaching of Islam.* [*In Preparation.*

BUDDHISM. 2 vols.
By Professor RHYS DAVIDS, LL.D., late Secretary of The Royal Asiatic Society.

PRIMITIVE OR NICENE CHRISTIANITY.
By JOHN SUTHERLAND BLACK, LL.D., Joint Editor of the *Encyclopædia Biblica.*

Other Volumes to follow.

SHINTO

THE ANCIENT RELIGION

OF JAPAN

By

W. G. ASTON, C.M.G., D.Lit.

LONDON

ARCHIBALD CONSTABLE & CO Ltd

16 JAMES STREET HAYMARKET

1907

Edinburgh : T. and A. Constable, Printers to His Majesty

CONTENTS

SHINTO: THE ANCIENT RELIGION OF JAPAN

CHAPTER I

INTRODUCTORY

Origins.—The Japanese are in the main a continental race. Their language and physical characteristics show conclusively that they come from Northern Asia, and geographical considerations indicate that Korea must have been their point of embarkation. Indeed a desultory emigration from Korea to Japan continued into historical times. When we say Northern Asia we exclude China. The racial affinity of the Japanese to the Chinese, of which we hear so often, really amounts to very little. It is not closer than that which unites the most distantly related members of the Indo-European family of nations. The Japanese themselves have no traditions of their origin, and it is now impossible to say what form of religion was professed by the

A

earliest immigrants. No inference can be drawn
from the circumstance that Sun-worship is
common to them with many North-Asiatic races.
The Sun is, or has been, worshipped almost every-
where. There is distinct evidence of a Korean
element in Shinto, but, with the little that we
know of the old native religion of that country,
anything like a complete comparison is impossible. Some have recognised a resemblance
between Shinto and the old state religion of
China, and it is true that both consist largely of
Nature-worship. But the two cults differ widely.
The Japanese do not recognise Tien (Heaven),
the chief Nature-deity of the Chinese, nor have
they anything to correspond to their Shangti—
a more personal ruler of the universe. The Sun
is masculine in China, feminine in Japan. The
Sun-goddess takes precedence of the Earth-god
in Japan, while in China Heaven and Earth
rank above the Sun and Moon. Some Chinese
traits are to be found in the old Shinto docu-
ments, but they are of later origin, and are
readily distinguishable from the native element.
A few similarities exist between Shinto and the
religion of the Ainus of Yezo, a savage race
which once occupied the main island of Japan.
But it is reasonable to suppose that in this case

the less civilised nation has borrowed from its more civilised neighbour and conqueror rather than *vice versa*. It is significant that the Ainu words for God, prayer, and offering, are taken from the Japanese. If the Malay or Polynesian element, which some have recognised in the Japanese race, has any existence, it has left no trace in religion. Such coincidences as may be noted between Shinto and oceanic religions, myths and practices are attributable to the like action of common causes rather than to inter-communication. The old Shinto owes little to any outside source. It is, on the whole, an independent development of Japanese thought.

Sources of Information.—The Japanese had no writing until the introduction of Chinese learning from Korea early in the fifth century of our era, and the first books which have come down to us date from the beginning of the eighth. One of these, called the *Kojiki* (712) is said to have been taken down from the lips of a man whose memory was well stored with the old myths and traditions of his country. He was perhaps one of the guild of 'reciters,' whose business it was to recite 'ancient words' at the ceremony which corresponds to our coronation. The *Kojiki* is a repertory of the old myths and legends, and, in the latter part, of the ancient history of Japan. The *Nihongi*, a work of similar scope, though based more on an existing written literature, was produced a few years later (720). It quotes numerous variants of the religious myths current at this time. There are voluminous and most learned commentaries on these two works written by Motoöri and Hirata in the eighteenth and nineteenth centuries. For the ritual of Shinto our chief source of information is the *Yengishiki*, a compilation made early in the tenth century. It contains, along with minute directions regarding offerings, ceremonies, etc., a series of the *norito* (litanies) used in Shinto worship which are of the highest interest, and of great, though unequal, antiquity.

The above-mentioned authorities give a tolerably complete account of the old state religion of Japan, sometimes called 'Pure Shinto,' in order to distinguish it from the Buddhicised cult of later times. Its palmy days may be taken to extend from the seventh to the twelfth century. Shinto, literally 'The Way of the Gods,' is a Chinese word, for which the Japanese equivalent is *Kami no michi*.

CHAPTER II

Kami is the ordinary Japanese word for God. It means primarily above, superior, and is applied to many other things besides deities, such as nobles, the authorities, the 'missus,' the hair of the head, the upper waters of a river, the part of Japan near Kiōto, etc. Height is in every country associated with excellence and divinity, no doubt because the first deities were the Sun and other Heavenly objects. We ourselves speak of the 'Most High' and use phrases like 'Good Heavens' which testify to a personification of the sky by our forefathers. But though Kami corresponds in a general way to 'God,' it has some important limitations. The Kami are high, swift, good, rich, living, but not infinite, omnipotent, or omniscient. Most of them had a father and mother, and of some the death is recorded. Motoöri, the great Shinto theologian, writing in

5

the latter part of the eighteenth century, says :—

'The term *Kami* is applied in the first place to the various deities of Heaven and Earth who are mentioned in the ancient records as well as to their spirits (*mi-tama*) which reside in the shrines where they are worshipped. Moreover, not only human beings, but birds, beasts, plants and trees, seas and mountains, and all other things whatsoever which deserve to be dreaded and revered for the extraordinary and preeminent powers which they possess, are called *Kami*. They need not be eminent for surpassing nobleness, goodness, or serviceableness alone. Malignant and uncanny beings are also called *Kami* if only they are the objects of general dread. Among *Kami* who are human beings I need hardly mention first of all the successive Mikados — with reverence be it spoken. . . . Then there have been numerous examples of divine human beings both in ancient and modern times, who, although not accepted by the nation generally, are treated as gods, each of his several dignity, in a single province, village, or family. . . . Amongst *Kami* who are not human beings, I need hardly mention Thunder [in Japanese *Naru Kami* or the Sounding God]. There are also the Dragon, the Echo [called in Japanese *Ko-dama* or the Tree Spirit] and the Fox, who are *Kami* by reason of their uncanny and fearful natures. The term *Kami* is applied in the *Nihongi* and *Manyōshiu* to the tiger and the wolf. Izanagi gave to the fruit of the peach, and to the jewels round his neck names which implied that they were *Kami*. . . . There are many cases of seas and mountains being called *Kami*.

It is not their spirits which are meant. The word was applied directly to the seas or mountains themselves as being very awful things.'

The Kami Beneficent.—The saying of the old Roman poet that 'Fear first made the Gods' does not hold good of Shinto. It is rather, as Schiller called the worship of the gods of Greece, a *Wonnedienst*, a religion inspired by love and gratitude more than by fear. The three greatest gods, viz. the Sun-goddess, the Food-goddess, and Ohonamochi (a god of Earth, the universal provider), are all beneficent beings, though they may send a curse when offended by the neglect of their worship or an insult to their shrines. Their worshippers come before them with gladness, addressing them as fathers, parents, or dear divine ancestors, and their festivals are occasions of rejoicing. But there are some malevolent or mischievous deities who have to be propitiated by offerings. The Fire-god, as is natural in a country where the houses are built of wood and great conflagrations are frequent, is one of these, and, in a lesser degree, the Thunder-god and the deity of the Rain-storm. The latter has, however, good points. He provides trees for the use of humanity, and rescues a maiden from being devoured by a great serpent.

SHINTO

Lafcadio Hearn's view that Shinto was at one time a religion of 'perpetual fear' is unsupported by evidence.

Classes of Kami. — Although the Kami are deficient in several of the attributes of the Christian God, they possess two essential qualities without which it would be impossible to recognise them as deities at all, viz., sentiency and superhuman power. The union of these ideas may be accomplished in two ways, first by attributing sense and will to the great elemental objects and phenomena, and secondly by applying to human and other living beings ideas of transcendent power derived from the contemplation of the mighty forces on whose operation we are daily and hourly dependent for our existence. We have therefore two classes of deities, Nature-gods and Man-gods, the first being the result of personification, the second of deification. It has been the generally received opinion that the Shinto gods belong to the latter rather than to the former of these two categories. Nine out of ten educated Japanese will declare with perfect sincerity that Shinto is ancestor-worship. Thus Mr. Daigoro Goh, a former secretary of the Japan Society, says:—'Shinto or ancestor-worship being the creed of the ancient inhabitants.' The same

8

view is held by some European scholars, notably the late Lafcadio Hearn, whose interesting and valuable work, *Japan, an Interpretation,* is greatly marred by this misconception. It is quite true that there is a large element of ancestor worship in modern Japanese religious practices, but a very little examination shows that all the great deities of the older Shinto are not Man, but Nature gods. Prominent among them we find the deities of the Sun, the Moon, the Earth, the Sea, the Rainstorm, Fire, Thunder, etc. And when the so-called ancestors of the Japanese race are not actually Nature-gods, they are usually the satellites or children of Nature-gods. In imitation of the Mikados who selected the Sun-goddess as their ancestral deity, the hereditary corporations or clans by whom in ancient times the Government of Japan, central and local, was carried on, chose for themselves, or perhaps invented, nature-deities, or their children or ministers, as their patron-gods, to whom special worship was paid. From this to a belief in their descent from him as an ancestor, the transition was easy. The same process has been observed in other countries. It was assisted by the habit of addressing the deity as father or parent, which, at first a metaphorical expression, came ultimately to be

9

understood in a more literal sense. These pseudo-ancestral deities were called Ujigami, that is to say 'surname-deities.' In later times the Ujigami ceased to be the patron-gods of particular families and became simply the local deities of the district where one was born. Children are presented to the Ujigami shortly after birth, and other important events, such as a change of residence, are announced to him. A deity of any class may become an Ujigami, and there have been cases of a Buddha attaining to this position. The cult of one's real forefathers, beginning with deceased parents, as in China, was hardly known in ancient Japan. Indeed there is but little trace of any religious worship of individual men in the Shinto of the *Kojiki* and *Nihongi*. Living Mikados were styled Kami, and spoken of as the 'Heavenly Grandchild' of the Sun-goddess. But their godship was more titular than real. It was much on a par with that of the Pope and Emperor who in the Middle Ages were called 'Deus in terris.' No miraculous powers were claimed for them beyond a vague general authority over the minor gods of Japan. Deceased Mikados were occasionally worshipped by their descendants, but whether there was anything in this so-called worship to distinguish it from the ordinary funeral or commemorative services there is nothing to show. They had no shrines, and no rituals in their honour are preserved in the Yengishiki collection. At a later period, the cult of deceased Mikados acquired a more definite character. They were prayed to for rain, to stay curses, to restore the Mikado's health, etc. They had shrines erected to them, the offerings at which were assimilated to those made to Nature-deities. The Mikado Ôjin, if we may believe an oracle delivered by himself, became an important War-god under the name of Hachiman. The Empress Jingō, the legendary conqueror of Korea, also received divine honours. At the present day, solemn services are held periodically in the Imperial Palace for the worship of all the dynasty.

Both categories of deities, Man and Nature gods, have three subdivisions according as they are deities of individuals, of classes, or of qualities. All these are exemplified in Shinto. The Sun-goddess represents an individual object; Kukuchi, the god of Trees, a class; and Musubi, the god of Growth, an abstract quality. Temmangu is a deified individual statesman, Koyane represents the Nakatomi clan or family, and Tajikara no wo (hand-strength-male) is a personified human quality.

Development of the Idea of God.—The Nature-gods of Shinto, as of other religions, are in the first place the actual material objects or phenomena regarded as living beings. Sometimes the personification proceeds no further. There are Mud and Sand deities which have no sex, and no mythical record beyond a bare mention. But in the case of others the same progressive humanising process that is to be observed elsewhere has already begun. The Sun is not only the brilliant heavenly being whose retirement to a cave leaves the world to darkness, she is a queen, a child, and a mother—in a miraculous fashion. She speaks, weaves, wears armour, sows seed, and does many other things which have nothing to do with her solar quality. At a still more recent stage—though not in the old records—she becomes an independent personage who rules the Sun, while with many worshippers at the present day her solar character is forgotten altogether, and she is considered merely as a great divine ancestor who dwells at Ise and exercises a providential guardianship over Japan. This line of development is familiar to us in other mythologies, the two stages of thought being often confounded. In Shakespeare's *Tempest*, Iris is at once the rainbow and an anthropomorphic messenger of the gods. Phoebus is not only the sun but a deity distinct from that luminary, though associated with it, as in the story of Phaeton. As the god of music and poetry, his solar function is not obvious. The same is true of the gods of the Vedas.

Impersonality of Shinto.—The faculty of imagination was not powerful with the ancient Japanese. It was active, and produced many deities of all classes. But they are very feebly characterised. Indeed, most of them may be said to have no characters at all. They are popularly reckoned at eighty myriads, or eight hundred myriads. Though this is a fanciful exaggeration, Shinto is a highly polytheistic religion, and numbers its deities by hundreds, even if we do not go back to that earlier period when the rocks, the trees, and the foam of water had all power of speech. There is a constant depletion in their ranks by the mere force of oblivion, while, on the other hand, new deities come into notice. Different gods are identified with one another, or the same deities may be split up like Musubi into a pair, or a number of distinct persons. The same deity at different places may have different ranks and attributes.

Spiritism.—The gods of ancient Shinto are, on the whole, as unspiritual beings as the gods of

13

Olympus. Their doings are modelled on those of living men and women, not on those of ghosts. When Izanagi followed his wife Izanami to the land of the dead he found there not a spirit, but a putrefying corpse. Ghosts are as absent from the *Kojiki* and *Nihongi* as they are from the Old Testament Scriptures. Herbert Spencer's ghost-theory of the origin of religion derives no support from the Japanese evidence. There is, however, a spiritual element in Shinto which demands notice. Some of the gods are represented as having *mitama* (august jewels or souls) which reside invisibly in their temples and are the means of communication between Heaven and this world. The Earth or Kosmos deity Ohona-mochi had a *mitama* (double) which appeared to him in a divine radiance illuminating the sea, and obtained from him a promise that, in considera-tion of the assistance the latter had rendered in reducing the world to order, he should have a shrine consecrated to him at Mimoro. Susa no wo's *mitama* was 'settled' at Susa in Idzumo. The element *tama* (soul) enters into the names of several deities. This implies a more or less spiritual conception of their nature. Sometimes we hear of two *mitama*, one of a gentle, the other of a violent nature.

14

There are only one or two cases of deceased men having mitama. In one of these the mitama takes the shape of a bird. Metamorphoses are frequently mentioned in the old legends.

Shekinah.—As in the analogous case of the Shekinah of Judaism, the doctrine of the mitama of gods apparently does not arise from that of the separability of the human soul and body. It seems rather to have been invented in order to smooth over the difficulty of conceiving how the gods of Heaven can exercise their power and hear and answer prayer in their shrines on earth. It may, however, owe something to the notion of separate human souls, which, though we do not find it in the older Japanese records, is familiar to races of a much lower degree of civilisation.

Immortality of the Soul.—This doctrine is nowhere directly taught in the Shinto books. There is a land of Yomi to which we are told that some of the gods retired at death. It is represented as inhabited by various personifications of death and disease, but not by human beings or their ghosts, though the phrase 'even pass of Yomi,' like the *facilis descensus Averni*, seems intended to express the facility with which all we mortal men find our way thither. In one passage of the *Nihongi*, Yomi is clearly no more than a metaphor for the grave. A brother of Jimmu Tenno, the first Mikado, is said to have gone to the 'Eternal Land' at his death, and in a poem of the Manyōshiu, a deceased Mikado is said to have ascended into heaven. The prehistoric custom of sacrificing wives and attendants at the tombs of dead sovereigns may be thought to imply a belief in their continued existence. But there are other motives for this practice than the wish to gratify the deceased by providing him with companions in the other world. The *norito* or rituals contain no reference to the immortality of the soul.

Shintai.—The mitama is represented in the shrine by a concrete object termed the Shintai or 'God-body.' It may be a mirror, a sword, a tablet with the god's name, a pillow, a spear, etc. A round stone, which is cheap and durable, is a very common Shintai. The god is sometimes represented as attaching himself to the Shintai, and may be even considered identical with it by the ignorant. The *mitama* and *shintai* are frequently confounded. The latter was in many cases originally an offering which, by long association, came ultimately to be looked upon as partaking in some measure of the divine nature.

Idols.—With a few unimportant exceptions,

Shinto has no idols. The Shintai is not in the least anthropomorphic. The pictures of the gods sold at shrines at the present day are due to Chinese or Buddhist influence.

Functions of Gods.—The two great classes of deities, Nature-gods and Man-gods, have a tendency mutually to encroach on each other's functions, so that ultimately they become assimilated under the one general term Kami. As we have seen above, the Sun-goddess does not confine herself to her function as a giver of light and heat, but does many things characteristic of a magnified human being. Susa no wo, the Rainstorm, provides mankind with useful trees. He and his wife are regarded as gods of wedlock. Inari, the Grain-god, is a comprehensive answerer of prayer from a petition for a good harvest to one for the restoration of stolen property. On the other hand, a genuine deified man like Temmangu may send rain in time of drought. An obscure deity, known as Suitengu, is worshipped in Tokio at the present day as a protector against the perils of the sea, burglary, and the pains of parturition. Almost any Kami, whatever his origin, may send rain, bestow prosperity in trade, avert sickness, cure sickness or sterility, and so on, without much discrimination of function.

CHAPTER III

Character of Japanese Myth.—Japanese myth covers much the same ground as the myths of other countries. We have the explanatory myth, invented in order to account for some custom or rite, some natural phenomenon, a name of a place or person, etc. There is an abundance of highly frivolous, revolting, childish, and unmeaning—to us at least—matter, and the various versions of the stories which have come down to us are often wholly inconsistent with one another. From the sketch of the mythical narrative which is given below, many details of this description have necessarily been omitted. There are, however, two leading ideas by which Japanese myth is redeemed from summary condemnation as a mere farrago of childish nonsense. In the first place, it is permeated by the conception of the so-called inanimate universe as being in reality instinct with sentient life. The old Shintoists had not

18

grasped the more general and philosophic notion of the Immanence of Deity in all things. With their limited scientific knowledge this was impossible. But they had the same idea in a more desultory, fragmentary way. To them, the Sun, the Wind, the Sea, were *Kami* who could hear and answer prayer, and exercise a providential care over mankind. But the synthesis of these and other aspects of nature and humanity into one divine whole is necessarily wanting. The second idea which inspires Japanese myth corresponds to our European notion of the divine right of kings, which, apart from the accident of heredity, is not such a negligible quantity as is sometimes supposed. The Mikados are represented as deriving their authority, whether as high-priests or sovereigns, from their ancestor, the Sun-goddess, and have, therefore, a divinely ordered right to the reverence and obedience of their subjects.

There is no summer and winter myth in the old records, no deluge myth, and no eclipse myth. The stars are strangely neglected. Earthquakes are hardly noticed. There is no Returning Saviour myth, and no Journey of the Dead, though the expressions 'Even Pass of Hades' and *Yaso-kumade* (eighty-road-windings, an alternative word for the land of Darkness) suggest that this idea was not unknown. The creation of mankind generally is not accounted for; but the origin of many of the ruling caste is ascribed to direct descent from the principal divinities, just as the Mikado is said to be descended from the Sun-goddess.

First Gods.—Four different first gods are mentioned by the various authorities. None of these ever attained to much importance. They were no doubt collected or invented with the purpose of eking out a genealogical tree for the greater divinities who came afterwards. One of these, called *Ame yudzuru hi ame no sagiri Kuni yudzuru tsuki Kuni no sagiri*, is described as the Heavenly Parent. But we know nothing more about him or her—the sex is doubtful—and it is impossible to regard this interminable title as the name of a real god, any more than we can think that Shakespeare's *honorificabilitudinitatibus* was ever meant for a genuine word. The derivation, however, shows that this, like the other first gods, was intended as a nature-deity. The four generations which follow consist of obscure personages, all of whom disappear at once from the record. Their names, too, are suggestive of nature, and more especially agriculture-

20

deities. In the sixth generation we find two deities, named *Kami-musubi* and *Taka-musubi*, *i.e.* High-growth and Divine-growth, who were of some importance in later times.

Izanagi and Izanami.—With these two deities Japanese myth really begins.

The *Nihongi* tells us that—

' Izanagi and Izanami stood on the floating bridge of Heaven (the rainbow) and held counsel together, saying " Is there not a country beneath ? " Thereupon they thrust down the " Jewel-Spear of Heaven," and groping about with it, found the ocean. The brine which dripped from the point of the spear coagulated and formed an island which received the name of Onogoro-jima or the " Self-Coagulating Island." The two deities thereupon descended and dwelt there. Accordingly they wished to be united as husband and wife, and to produce countries. So they made Onogoro-jima the pillar of the centre of the land.'

The *Kojiki* says that Izanagi and Izanami were commanded by all the heavenly deities ' to regulate and fully consolidate' the floating land beneath. But all the accounts, the *Kojiki* included, proceed to represent the islands of Japan as having been generated by them in the ordinary manner. We have therefore three distinct conceptions of creation in Japanese myth—first, as generation in the most literal sense; second, as reducing to order; and third, as growth (*Musubi*).

'The two deities having descended on Onogoro jima erected there an eight-fathom house with an august central pillar. Then Izanagi addressed Izanami, saying, "Let me and thee go round the heavenly august pillar, and having met at the other side, let us become united in wedlock." This being agreed to, he said, "Do thou go round from the left, and I will go round from the right." When they had gone round, Izanami spoke first and exclaimed, "How delightful! I have met a lovely youth." Izanagi then said, "How delightful! I have met a lovely maiden." Afterwards he said, "It was unlucky for the woman to speak first." The child which was the first offspring of their union was the Hiruko (leech-child), which at the age of three was still unable to stand upright, and was therefore placed in a reed-boat and sent adrift.'

Izanagi and Izanami then procreated the islands of Japan with a number of other gods, among whom were *Iha-tsuchi-biko* (rock-earth-prince), *Oho-ya-biko* (great-house-prince), the Wind-gods, a variety of marine deities, *Ame no Mikumari* (the heavenly water distributor), the god of Moors (who is also the god of Herbs and Grasses), the god of Trees, the gods of Mountains and Valleys, and the goddess of Food. The last deity to be produced was the god of Fire, *Kagu-tsuchi*, also called *Ho-musubi* (Fire-growth). In giving birth to him, Izanami was burnt so that she sickened and lay down. From her vomit, fæces, and urine were born deities which personify the elements of metal, water, and clay. When Izanami died, Izanagi, in his grief and rage, drew his sword and slew Kagu-tsuchi, thereby generating a number of other deities, two of whom, named Take-mika-tsuchi and Futsunushi, were favourite objects of worship in later times.

The creation of the Sun and Moon is variously accounted for. Some say that they were the children of Izanagi and Izanami, others that they were born from the lustrations of Izanagi when he returned from Yomi. A third child, Susa no wo, the boisterous and unruly Rain-storm god, was produced at the same time.

When Izanami died she went to the Land of Yomi, whither she was followed by her husband. But as she had already eaten of the food of that region, he could not bring her back with him. She forbade him to look on her, but he persisted and saw that she was already a putrid corpse. Izanami then complained that he had put her to shame, and caused him to be pursued by the Ugly Females of Hades and other personifications of corruption and disease who dwelt there. She herself had become Death personified. Izanagi,

in his flight, flung down various objects which
delayed his pursuers—a well-known incident
of myth—until he reached the Even Pass of
Hades, where he pronounced the formula of
divorce.

When Izanagi returned to earth he bathed in
the sea in order to remove the pollution incurred
by his visit to Yomi, and in so doing produced a
number of deities, some of whom are Ocean-gods
and others associated with the ancient Japanese
ceremonies of religious purification.

Susa no wo and the Sun-Goddess.—Susa no wo
(the Rain-storm god) was at first appointed to rule
the Sea, but he preferred to join his mother,
Izanami, in Hades, and was accordingly despatched thither by his father. Before taking
his departure, however, he ascended to heaven
to take leave of his elder sister Amaterasu, the
Sun-goddess. All the mountains and rivers shook,
and every land and country quaked as he passed
upwards. Amaterasu, in alarm, armed herself as
a warrior with sword and bow, stamped her feet
into the hard ground up to her thighs, kicking
away the earth like rotten snow, and, confronting
him like a valiant man, challenged him to declare
the reason of his coming. Susa no wo protested
that it was only a friendly visit, and as a proof of

his good intentions proposed that they should produce children between them by each one crunching
in his mouth and spurting out fragments of the
sword and jewels worn by the other. One of the
children thus born was called *Masaya a katsu
kachi hayahi ama no oshihomimi*, the forefather
of the present Imperial dynasty. There were
seven others who figure largely in the genealogies
of the Japanese nobility.

But the true nature of the Rain-storm god was
not long repressed. He destroyed his sister's rice-
fields, defiled the sacred hall where she was cele-
brating the harvest festival, and flung a piebald
colt that had been flayed backwards into the
sacred weaving-room where the garments of the
gods were woven. The Sun-goddess had borne
his previous outrages with calmness and forbear-
ance, but this last (a malicious magical practice ?)
was beyond endurance. She retired in disgust
and shut herself up in the Rock-cave of Heaven,
leaving the world to darkness. This proceeding
of Amaterasu was followed by dire results. 'The
voices of the evil deities were like unto the flies
in the fifth moon as they swarmed, and a myriad
portents of woe arose.' The gods, in consternation,
held an assembly in the dry bed of the River of
Heaven (the Milky Way) to devise means for

inducing her to emerge from the cave, and a number of expedients were adopted which were evidently borrowed from the ritual of the time when the myth became current. The deities who were specially concerned with this duty are obvious counterparts of the actual officials of the Mikado's Court, and included a prayer-reciter, an offering-provider, a mirror-maker, a jewel-maker, a diviner, with—according to some accounts—many others. All this is most convenient for the genealogists of later times. Amaterasu at length reappeared, to the great delight of everybody. Susa no wo was fined in a thousand tables of offerings and expelled from Heaven. Before proceeding to Yomi, he went down to Earth. Here he appears in a totally new character as the Perseus of a Japanese Andromeda, whom he rescues from a huge serpent, having first intoxicated the monster. Of course they are married and have numerous children. Her name, Inada-hime (rice-land-lady), is probably not without significance as that of the wife of a Rain-storm god. Another story represents him as the murderer of the Food-goddess, who had offended him by producing viands for his entertainment from various parts of her body. But a different version ascribes this crime to the Moon-god, and gives it as the reason why the

Sun-goddess refused to have any further relations with him. This, of course, explains why the two luminaries are not seen together.

Here it may be pointed out that, notwithstanding the anthropomorphic character of many of the above details it is evidently the sun itself which is concealed in the Rock-cave. Modern Euhemerists deny this. But the evidence is far too strong to be disregarded. Her names, Amaterasu (Heaven Shining-one) and Hirume (Sunfemale), are conclusive on this point. The modern commentator Motoöri agrees, or rather maintains, that Amaterasu is the very sun which we see in heaven. Those Japanese who in the twentieth century talk of the imperial visit to Ise as ancestor-worship are sorely puzzled to justify their position. Imbued with the philosophy of China and the science of Europe, they naturally find it difficult to understand how the Mikado can be really descended from the sun. Some resort to the Euhemeristic theory that she was a mortal Empress who lived in a place on earth called Takanna no hara (plain-of-high-heaven), and speak of rice-culture and the art of weaving being known in her reign.

The myth of the Sun-goddess and Susa no wo is the central pivot on which the old mythology turns. All that precedes may be regarded as a sort of genealogical introduction, and the subsequent narrative as an epilogue designed to complete the connexion between the living Mikados and their celestial ancestor.

Ohonamochi.—One of Susa no wo's children was an Earth-god named Ohonamochi (great-name-possessor), who is at this day a very important deity. The *Kojiki* relates his adventures at great length. He was badly treated by his eighty elder brothers, but assisted by a hare to whom he had rendered service. He went down to the land of Yomi, where he married the daughter of Susa no wo. Susa no wo imposed tasks upon him which by his wife's assistance he performed successfully, and ultimately made his escape, taking her with him. The Yomi of this narrative has little that is characteristic of the abode of the Dead. Ohonamochi is frequently referred to as the 'God who made the land,' and his various names show that he is an Earth-god. He was assisted in reducing the country to order by his own *mitama* or double, and by a dwarf-god called Sukuna-bikona, who came from beyond the sea and is credited with having instructed mankind in the arts of medicine and brewing. Ohonamochi had a numerous progeny by various mothers. Among them were the Harvest-god and the Food-goddess. The *Kojiki* gives a genealogy of them and their descendants, most of whom are wholly unknown to us.

Ninigi.—Meanwhile the Sun-Goddess became desirous of establishing the rule of her own grandchild Ninigi, son of Masaya a katsu, in Japan. After several fruitless attempts to prepare the country for his reception by purging it of the swarms of evil deities which infested it, two gods named Take-mika-tsuchi (Thunder?) and Futsunushi (Fire?) were sent to summon Ohonamochi to yield over his authority. After some demur he did so, and Ninigi was accordingly despatched to earth, accompanied by a long train of attendants who provide further material for the genealogists. They descended on a mountain in Kiushiu. Here Ninigi took to wife a Mountain-god's daughter, named Konohana Sakuya-hime (the lady who blossoms like the flowers of the trees), rejecting as too ugly her elder sister Iha-naga-hime. (the rock-long-lady). The latter, indignant at this slight, uttered a curse:—'The race of visible men shall change swiftly like the flowers of the trees, and shall decay and pass away.' Hence the shortness of human life. By Konohana Ninigi had three children. The eldest,

Ho no Susori, became a fisherman, the second son, Hohodemi, a hunter.

Ho no Susori once proposed to his brother to exchange their respective callings. Hohodemi accordingly gave over to his elder brother his bow and arrows and received a fish-hook in return. But neither of them profited by the exchange, so Ho no Susori gave back to his brother the bow and arrows and demanded from him the fish-hook.

Hohodemi, however, had in the meantime lost it in the sea. He took his sword and forged from it a number of new fish-hooks which he piled up in a winnowing tray and offered to his brother by way of compensation. But the latter would have none but his own, and demanded it so vehemently of Hohodemi as to grieve him bitterly. Hohodemi went down to the sea-shore and stood there lamenting, when there appeared to him the Old Man of the Sea, by whose advice he descended into the sea-depths to the abode of the god of the Sea, a stately palace with lofty towers and battlements. Before the gate there was a well, and over the well grew a thick-branching cassia tree into which Hohodemi climbed. The Sea-god's daughter Toyo-tama-hime (rich-jewel-maiden) then came out from the palace to draw water.

She saw Hohodemi's face reflected in the well, and returning within reported to her father that she had seen a beautiful youth in the tree which grew by the well. Hohodemi was courteously received by the Sea-god, Toyo-tama-hiko (rich-jewel-prince), who, when he heard his errand, summoned before him all the fishes of the sea and made inquiry of them for the lost fish-hook, which was eventually discovered in the mouth of the Tai. Toyo-tama-hiko delivered it to Hoho-demi, telling him when he gave it back to his brother to say, ' a hook of poverty, a hook of ruin, a hook of downfall,' to spit twice, and to hand it over with averted face.

Hohodemi married the Sea-god's daughter Toyo-tama-hime and remained with her for three years. He then became home-sick and returned to the upper world. On the beach where he came to land, he built for his wife, who was soon to follow, a parturition house which he thatched with cormorant's feathers. The roofing was still unfinished when she arrived, riding on a great tortoise. She went straight into the hut, begging her husband not to look at her. But Hohodemi's curiosity was too strong for him. He peeped in, and behold ! his wife had become changed into a *wani* (sea-dragon) eight fathoms long. Deeply indignant at the disgrace put upon her, Toyo-tama-hime abandoned her new-born child to the care of her sister, and barring behind her the sea-path in such a way that from that day to this all communication between the realms of land and sea has been cut off, returned hastily to her father's palace.

Hohodemi's troubles with his elder brother were renewed on his arrival home. He was obliged to use against him two talismans given him by his father-in-law. One of these had the virtue of making the tide flow and submerge Ho no Susori and thus compel him to sue for mercy (another account says that Hohodemi whistled and thereby raised the wind and the sea). Then by a second talisman the tide was made to recede and Ho no Susori's life was spared. He yielded complete submission to his younger brother and promised that he and his descendants to all generations would serve Hohodemi and his successors as mimes and bondservants. The *Nihongi* adds that in that day it was still customary for the Hayato (or Imperial guards), who were descended from Ho no Susori, to perform a mimic dance before the Mikados, the descendants and successors of Hohodemi, in which the drowning struggles of their ancestor were represented.

MYTH

There are several features in this story which betray a recent origin and foreign influences. A comparatively advanced civilisation is indicated by the sword and fish-hook forged of iron. The institution of the Hayato as Imperial Guards belongs to a period not very long antecedent to the date of the *Nihongi* and *Kojiki*. The palace of the sea-depths and its Dragon-king are of Chinese, and therefore of recent origin.

One of Hohodemi's grandchildren was Jimmu Tennō, who is usually reckoned the first human sovereign of Japan. He was the youngest of four brothers and his selection as heir shows that primogeniture, though to some extent acknowledged in Ancient Japan, was by no means the universal rule. At the age of forty-five he started from Kiushiu, which had been the home of the Imperial family since Ninigi descended there, on an expedition for the conquest of the central part of Japan, known as Yamato. This event is dated in B.C. 667, 1,792, 470 years after the descent of Ninigi from heaven. He finally succeeded in establishing his capital there in B.C. 660. From this date Japanese history is usually said to begin. In reality there is no genuine history of Japan for one thousand years more. The chronology for all this period is a colossal fraud

C

and there is abundant intrinsic evidence that the narrative itself is no better than legend when it is not absolute fiction. There is, however, much to be learned from it of the beliefs and customs of the ancient Japanese.

The descent of the Imperial dynasty from a Sea-god has been noted as an auspicious omen for the development of Japan as a great naval power.

CHAPTER IV

NATURE-GODS OF INDIVIDUALS AND OF CLASSES

SOME of the principal gods have already been introduced in the preceding chapter. Let us now consider them separately, according to the classification already indicated (p. 8). It is often difficult to say whether a nature-god represents an individual object or phenomenon, or a class. This is chiefly owing to the circumstance that Japanese, like other Far-Eastern languages, habitually neglects the distinction between the singular and the plural number. The idea of making verbs and adjectives agree in number with the substantives to which they belong does not seem to have occurred to these nations, and, even in the case of nouns and pronouns, plural particles are very sparingly used. *Yama no Kami*, for example, may mean either God of the Mountain, God of Mountains, Gods of the Mountain, or Gods of Mountains.

Amaterasu, the **Sun-Goddess**.—The Sun-goddess belongs unmistakably to the first class, viz., that of individual objects personified. She is much the most prominent member of the Shinto Pantheon, and is described as the Ruler of Heaven and unrivalled in dignity. She wears royal insignia, and is surrounded by a court. The chief religious ceremony of state was in her honour. Yet she is not what we should call a Supreme Deity. She is by no means an autocrat. Even in heaven, which she is supposed to govern, there is a Council of the Gods which decides important matters. In some myths she has a formidable rival in *Taka musubi*, a god of Growth.

The ascription of the female sex to the deity of the Sun has more meaning than might be supposed. Women held a far more important and independent position in ancient Japan than they did at a later time when Chinese ideas of their subjection became prevalent. Several of the ancient Mikados were women. Old Chinese books call Japan the 'Queen-country.' Women chieftains are frequently mentioned. Some of the most important monuments of the old literature were the work of women.

Like the Sun-Gods of ancient Greece and Egypt, Amaterasu possesses a sacred bird, the Yatagarasu, or eight-hand-crow. An old Japanese dictionary identifies this bird, rightly in my opinion, with the Yangwu or Sun-crow of Chinese myth. The Yangwu is a bird of a red colour with three legs which inhabits the sun. The Yatagarasu was lent by the Sun-goddess to Jimmu Tennō as a guide to his expedition against the tribes who then held the province of Yamato. A noble Japanese family claimed descent from this bird.

The Sun-goddess is represented in the shrine of Ise by her shintai or token, which is called the Yatakagami or eight-hand mirror. It is related that when she sent down her grandchild Ninigi to rule the earth, she gave him this mirror with the injunction: 'Regard this mirror exactly as our mitama (soul) and reverence it as if reverencing us.' At this day the Yatakagami is held in high reverence. It is kept in a bag of brocade which is never opened or repaired, a new one being added on the top of its predecessor when the latter is too much worn for further use The *Nihongi* calls it the 'Great-God of Ise.'

Amaterasu is not the only Sun-deity of Japanese myth. We hear of a Waka-hirume (young-sun-female) who is no doubt a personification of the morning sun, and of a Nigi-haya-hi (gentle, swift-sun). The latter is said to have come down from heaven in a heavenly rock-boat, and to have become the chieftain of one of the tribes subdued by Jimmu Tennō. He may, however, have been a human being named as a compliment after the Sun. This proceeding is not unknown in Japanese history. But I rather suspect that he is a real Sun-god. Then there is the Hiruko mentioned at p. 22 as the first-born of all the deities. Now Hiruko, though written with Chinese characters which mean leech-child, may also mean Sun-male-child, and this is obviously its proper meaning. The Hiruko was a male Sun-deity who afterwards became obsolete. For some unknown reason Hiruko has been identified with a popular modern deity named Yebisu, who has to all appearance nothing to do with either the sun or the leech. He is pictured as an angler with a fish dangling at the end of his line. He has a smiling countenance and wears old Japanese costume. Merchants pray to him for success in trade.

At the present day the title Amaterasu no oho-kami (the great deity who illumines heaven) is generally replaced by its Chinese equivalent Tenshōdaijin. The meaning of the latter is less clear to the uneducated, who forget that she has any connection with the sun. Sun-worship, however, proceeds independently. Women and children especially call it by the respectful name of Otentō sama, without attribution of sex, with no formal cult, and no myth, but endowed with moral attributes, punishing the wicked and rewarding the just. Dr. Griffis describes a scene which he witnessed in Tokio when, late one afternoon, Otentō sama, which had been hidden behind clouds for a fortnight, shone out on the muddy streets. In a moment scores of people rushed out of their houses, and with faces westward began prayer and worship before the great luminary. Many people keep awake all night on the last day of the year so as to worship the rising sun on the first day of the New Year.

Tsuki-yomi.—The Sun being feminine, Tsuki-yomi, the moon-deity, is naturally masculine. Though he has shrines at Ise and other places, he occupies a far less prominent place in Japanese myth and cult than his elder sister Amaterasu.

Susa no wo.—The true character of this deity had been forgotten by the Japanese themselves until he was shown by an American scholar, Dr. Buckley of Chicago, to be a personification of the Rain-storm. The generally accepted etymology of his name derives it from a verb *susamu*, to be impetuous. This accords well

with his character as described in the *Kojiki*
and *Nihongi*. Mr. B. H. Chamberlain translates
by 'the Impetuous Male,' and he may be correct.
But there is a town in Idzumo called Susa where
this god had a shrine, and it seems possible that
it was from this that he took his name.

Star-Gods are few and unimportant in Shinto.

Earth-worship. — The direct worship of the
Earth is well-known in Japan. At the present
day, when a new building is erected or new
rice-land brought under cultivation, the ground
is solemnly propitiated by a ceremony called
Ji-matsuri or earth-worship. Localities were personified under names which recall Erin, Britannia,
Dea Roma, etc. Such deities were called Kuni-
dama, country or province spirit. The greatest
of these, and one of the three greatest gods of
Shinto, is Ohonamochi. His shrine at Kitsuki
in Idzumo is known as the Taisha or great
shrine, and he has numerous other shrines, called
Sannō or Hiye, in all parts of the country. In
his case the deification has proceeded beyond the
mere personification of the soil. Legend represents him as the maker of the land, not the
land itself, and in modern times nobody thinks
of him as an Earth-god. His various names,
however, show conclusively that he is as much

an earth-deity as the Greek Gaia, who, like him, was 'one shape of many names.' Lafcadio Hearn would make him out to be the god of the dead, though there are already two other rulers of Hades, and Dr. Buckley thinks that he is a Moon-god. With Ohonamochi there is associated his minister, an important deity named Kotoshiro-nushi, and a dwarf-god, Sukuna-bikona, who is credited with the invention of medicine, magic, and the art of brewing sake.

Another Earth-god is Asuha, an obscure personage, who is supposed to be the deity of the courtyard. Mud, sand, and clay are deified under the names of Uhijini, Suhijini, and Hani-yasu-hime, the last name meaning clay-easy (in the sense of plastic) lady. Clay was deified because it supplied the material for the domestic cooking furnace, a defence against the encroaches of that unruly power, fire.

Mountain-Gods.—Most mountains have their deity, which is sometimes conceived of as the mountain itself, at others as a god of the mountain. Mountain gods do not take high rank in the Shinto Pantheon. They were propitiated before trees were cut for building purposes.

Earthquake-Gods are little heard of. But any god might cause an earthquake if offended.

Sea-Gods.—The chief Sea-gods of Shinto are Sokotsu-wata-dzumi (bottom-sea-body), Nakatsu-wata-dzumi (middle-sea-body), and Uhatsu-wata-dzumi (upper-sea-body), three deities produced from Izanagi's ablutions in the sea when he returned from Hades. They are also represented as forming one deity. So that we have here an example — not the only one — of a Japanese Trinity. They have a famous shrine at Sumi-yoshi near Osaka, and are much prayed to for safety from shipwreck and for fair winds.

Another Sea-god, Toyotama hiko, has been already mentioned above (p. 31).

River-Gods are represented as dragons or serpents. The resemblance of a river with its winding serpentine course, and its mysterious motion without legs, to a great serpent, has struck mankind in many countries. The Chinese, the Mexicans, and the Semitic nations concur in associating water with the serpent. It is mostly the maleficent aspect of rivers that is thus symbolised. There are traditions in Japanese legend of human sacrifices to rivers.

Rain-Gods.—Special Rain-gods are mentioned in the old myths, but in practice any deity might be appealed to for aid in time of drought.

Wells. — There are sacred wells from which

the water required in sacrifice was drawn. The water itself was made a female deity under the name of Midzuha no me. At the present day, the ordinary well or stream from which water is taken for domestic purposes is propitiated early on the morning of the New Year by small offerings.

Wind - Gods. — Sometimes one Wind - god is spoken of, sometimes two, one masculine and one feminine. They were formerly much prayed to for good harvests. One legend calls them the Ame no mihashira and Kuni no mihashira (august pillar of heaven and august - pillar of earth). The idea that the winds support the sky is not unknown in other mythologies.

Take - mika - dzuchi and **Futsunushi.** — The proper character of these two deities is not quite clear. The name of the former is frequently written with Chinese characters which imply that he is a Thunder-god, and Futsunushi is probably a god of fire, perhaps more specifically the lightning. They are constantly associated in legend and worship. They were sent down from heaven together to prepare Japan for the advent of Ninigi, the Sun-Goddess's grandchild, and their shrines at Kashima and Katori, on the east coast of Japan, are adjacent to one another.

At the present day they are universally recognised as War-gods. This accounts for the choice of Kashima and Katori as the names of recently-launched battle-ships of the Imperial Japanese Navy. These deities also predict the weather. The Japanese equivalent of old Moore's Almanac is the Kashima no Kotofure, *i.e.* notification from Kashima.

There is another Thunder-god called Ikadzuchi (dread father) or Naru Kami (sounding-god).

Fire-Gods.—*Kagutsuchi*, mentioned above (p. 22), is the chief fire-deity. He is also known as Ho-musubi (fire-growth), and his shrine stands on the summit of the high hill of Atago near Kioto. Hence the name Atago-Sama by which he is usually called. Hill-shrines are dedicated to him at the chief cities of Japan; and he is believed, when duly propitiated, to preserve them from conflagration. In the old State religion the god and fire are regarded as identical.

The sacrificial fire was deified, and also the *Nihabi*, a fire kindled with the object of producing sunshine. Both in ancient and modern times the domestic cooking-furnace has been considered as a deity.

Ukemochi, the Food-goddess, is one of the two great gods worshipped at Ise, the Sun - goddess

44

being the other. There is a tendency in modern times to identify her with Inari, a male grain-deity. Shrines of Inari are to be seen in every village, and even in many houses. They may be recognised by two figures of foxes which stand before them. These animals are thought by many to be the god himself, and small offerings of such food as is thought acceptable to foxes are placed before them. Shinto scholars say that they are only the god's attendants or messengers. But grain is often represented by an animal in other mythologies, and possibly this may be the case in Shinto also. Inari is much invoked by the peasant to grant him good crops, but as is so often the case, his proper agricultural character is frequently forgotten, and he is appealed to for help in all imaginable difficulties, as for the cure of small-pox or the discovery of a thief.

There are several harvest-gods not very clearly distinguished from the grain-deities. One of these, as well as Ukemochi, is said to be the child of Ohonamochi, the great Earth-god.

Tree-Gods.—Trees of great size and age are worshipped in almost every village in Japan. They are girt with honorary cinctures of straw-rope, and have tiny shrines erected before them. Other sacred trees are not themselves gods, but only offerings to the deities before whose shrines they are planted. Orchard trees are the object of a quaint ceremony which has its counterpart in many other places, Devonshire amongst the number, of cajoling or intimidating the trees into bearing good crops. In Japan one man climbs the tree, while another stands at the bottom with an axe, threatening to cut it down if it does not promise to bear plentifully. The man above responds that it will do so. Perhaps, however, the pleasure of acting a little drama has more to do with such customs than any real belief in their efficacy.

We also meet with a Kukunochi (trees-father) and a Kaya nu hime (reed-lady). Their worship was probably prompted by gratitude for their providing materials for house - building and thatching.

A House-God named Yabune is mentioned in one of the old rituals. A certain sanctity attaches to the Daikoku-bashira, or central pillar of the house, corresponding to our king-post. There is also a Gate-god (or gods), who guards the dwelling against the entrance of evil things, and, in modern times, a God of the Privy.

THE GODS

Izanagi and Izanami.—I have little doubt that these deities (see above, p. 21) were suggested by the Yin and Yang, or male and female principles, of Chinese philosophy. They were probably introduced into Japanese myth in order to account for the existence of the Sun-goddess and other deities, and to link them together by a common parentage. Their names are supposed to be connected with a verb, *izanafu,* to invite, and to refer to their mutual invitation to become husband and wife. They are not important in ritual.

Musubi means growth or production. In the old myths there are two Musubi deities, viz. Taka-musubi and Kamu-musubi (high-growth and divine-growth). It is not difficult to conjecture that ‘high’ and ‘divine’ were originally nothing more than laudatory epithets of one and the same personage. Poetry recognises only one God. In later times there were no fewer than eight Musubi who had shrines in the precincts of the Imperial palace. The worship of this god is now much neglected.

Kuni-toko-tachi.—Nothing is really known of this deity. The name means literally ‘land (or

47

earth)-eternal-stand,' and I offer as a mere conjecture that he is a personification of the durable
character of the earth. The circumstance that
he is the first god of the *Nihongi* myth led to his
receiving a prominence in later times which is
justified by nothing in the older religion. There
was an abortive attempt to make of him a sort of
Supreme Deity, and to substitute his worship for
that of the Food-goddess at Ise.

<h3 style="text-align:center">DEIFIED INDIVIDUAL MEN</h3>

Though all the greater gods of the old Shinto
were Nature-gods, we cannot affirm that none of
the numerous obscure deities mentioned in the
Kojiki and *Nihongi* were deified individual men.
The impulse to exalt human beings to the rank
of deity has always existed, and may have left
traces in the older Shinto, though the evidence
that this was so in any particular case is not
forthcoming.

Take-minakata, the god of Suha, in the province of Shinano, *may* be a deity of this class.
He was a son of Ohonamochi, who refused allegi-
ance to the Sun-goddess and fled to Suha, where
he was obliged to surrender. Tradition says that
the present high priests of his shrine are his
direct descendants. They are held to be his

incarnation, and are called Ikigami or 'live deities.' There are at the present day shrines to Suha Sama in many parts of Japan.

Hachiman is not mentioned in the *Kojiki* or *Nihongi*. His history is a curious one. The original place of his worship was Usa in Kiushiu, near the Straits of Shimonoseki, an old, perhaps the oldest, Shinto centre of Japan. He first came into notice in 720, when he helped to repel a piratical descent by Koreans. At a somewhat later period he became associated with the great Minamoto family, and attained to popularity as a War-god. But his cult is deeply tinctured with Buddhism. In his oracles he calls himself by the Buddhist title of Bosatsu (Boddhisattwa), something like our 'saint,' and ordains humanitarian festivals for the release of living things, a thoroughly Buddhist institution, and quite incongruous with his character as a Japanese Mars. It is explained that the reason for his deification as a War-god is that he was an unborn child in his mother Jingo's womb when she achieved her famous conquest of Korea. His identification with the Emperor Ôjin, however, dates from long after he became popular.

Temmangu, the God of Learning and Caligraphy. If we pass over the honours paid to

living and dead Mikados as of doubtful religious
quality, the first genuine deified human being on
the Shinto record is Sugahara Michizane, who
was raised to divine rank under the name of
Temmangu. Michizane was born in 845. His
family had a hereditary reputation for learning,
and traced its descent from the Sun-goddess
herself. His erudition gained him high rank in
the government, and a system of national education which he established acquired for him the
gratitude of the people, who called him the
'Father of letters.' But owing to the calumnies
of a rival he was banished to Kiushiu, where he
died in exile. Great calamities followed, which
were attributed to the wrath of Michizane's ghost,
and it was not until his sentence had been for-
mally cancelled, shrines erected, and other
honours paid him that it ceased to plague his
enemies and the nation. The story has come
down to us enriched with a profuse embroidery
of legendary details drawn from Buddhist and
Chinese sources.

Temmangu is, or was until recently, one of the
most widely worshipped of Shinto deities, especially by pedagogues and school-boys. In 1820,
there were twenty-five shrines to him in Yedo
and its neighbourhood. His cult was probably

suggested, and was certainly promoted, by the corresponding Chinese honours to Confucius.

Later Deifications.—In the Kojiki and Nihongi, a sort of titular divinity is ascribed to some of the Mikados. It was not until a later period that they had shrines or regular offerings. Chief among deified Mikados are Jimmu, Jingo, and Kwammu, the founder of Kioto. Takechi no Sukune, Jingo's chief counsellor; Prince Yamato-dake, the legendary hero who, in the second century of our era, subdued the eastern parts of Japan to the Mikado's rule; Nomi no Sukune, the patron deity of wrestlers; Hitomaro, the poet and Sotoörihime, the poetess, though treated as ordinary human beings in the old records, were deified in subsequent times. Quasi-divine honours are paid to Iyeyasu, the founder of the Tokugawa dynasty of Shōguns, and to many other distinguished men. Strange to say, a kind of religious cult is rendered to remarkable criminals, such as the famous robber Kumazaka Chōhan, and to Nishi no Buntaro, who in our own day assassinated the Minister of Education, Mori Arinori, because he raised with his walking-stick a curtain which screened off part of the shrine of Ise from vulgar gaze.

SHINTO

In the older Shinto, gods of types or classes occupy a fairly prominent position. They represent the hereditary corporations by which the government of Japan was carried on in early times. The officials of the Mikado's Court had their mythical counterparts in the ministers of the Sun-goddess, who were supposed to be their ancestors. Thus the Nakatomi family, who besides holding other high offices, were the recognised vicars of the Mikado in the discharge of his priestly functions, traced their descent from Koyane, a deity who, by reading a liturgy in honour of the Sun-goddess, helped to entice her from the dark Rock-cave of heaven. The Imbe, who provided the offerings for the state Shinto ceremonies, recognised as their ancestor a god called Futo-dama (great offering), who fulfilled the same office in heaven. Uzume, the Dread Female of heaven, had descendants in the female officials of the palace. There is a *norito* in her honour, in which she is besought to preserve order among the courtiers of all ranks. May we not trace a relationship between her and our own 'Dread Female' deity, Mrs. Grundy? The mirror-makers of the palace had their proto-

THE GODS

type in Ishikoridome, the jewellers in Toyotama
(rich-jewel), and so on.

GODS OF HUMAN QUALITIES

Students of Far-Eastern mythology and literature have observed the feeble grasp of personality
which distinguishes them from the similar pro-
ducts of the Western mind.[1] They are characterised by a certain poverty of imagination which
is manifested in various directions, and more
especially by the almost total absence of personified abstractions of human qualities. We look in
vain for such conceptions as Age, Youth, Love,
Fear, Patience, Hope, Charity, and a host of other
personified qualities. Ta-jikara no wo (hand-
strength-male) is one of the few examples of this
class. He it was who, when the Sun-goddess
partly opened the door of the Rock-cave to
which she had retired, took her by the hand and
dragged her out. But he is little worshipped,
and indeed is only a poetical adjunct to the
mythical narrative. In this respect he greatly
resembles the Kratos and Bia of Hesiod and
Æschylus.

Phallic Gods.—Far more important are the
Sahe no Kami, or phallic deities. Their symbols

[1] See Percival Lowell's *Soul of the Far East.*

53

were a familiar sight by the roadsides and at crossings in ancient Japan. They might be seen even in the busy thoroughfares of the capital itself. At first representatives of tho procreative, life-giving power, they were used as magical appliances for promoting fertility. But they became symbolical of life generally—the enemy of death and disease—and, on the well-known principle of magic that the symbol possesses something of the actual physical virtue of the thing which it represents, were employed as prophylactics against death and pestilence. For their services in this capacity they were deified. Their cult has long ago disappeared from the state religion, but it still lingers in the out-of-the-way parts of Eastern Japan.

CHAPTER V

In ancient Japan, the sacred and the secular were imperfectly differentiated from one another. The Department of Shinto was simply a Government bureau. Miya meant equally shrine and palace. Matsuri, a Shinto festival, is the same word that we also find in Matsurigoto, government. The Mikado was at once the high priest and the sovereign of the nation. In the oldest legends he appears frequently in a sacerdotal capacity, and, even at the present day, he takes a personal part in some of the Shinto rites. Only last year he went to Ise to perform the ceremony of Nihiname, or tasting the first rice of the new harvest after making an offering of it to the Sun-goddess. But even in the oldest records there occur instances of his deputing his sacerdotal functions. Jimmu Tenno is said to have appointed Michi No Omi (minister-of-the-way) as ' Ruler of a festival.' The rubrics of the *norito*

55

(rituals) show that they were intended to be read by a deputy and not by the Mikado in person.

The Nakatomi.—The chief officials of the Bureau of Shinto were appointed from the hereditary clan or family of the Nakatomi, from which the principal ministers of state and the Imperial Consorts were also selected. The great Fujiwara House, so famous in later times, was a branch of the Nakatomi.

The Imbe had the duty of preparing the offerings for sacrifice. Their name, which includes the word 'imi,' signifying religious abstinence, purity, refers to the strict avoidance of ritual pollution which was incumbent on them in the discharge of this function.

The Urabe were diviners attached to the bureau of Shinto.

Kannushi is the ordinary word for a Shinto priest. The Kannushi are not celibates, and are not distinguishable from the laity except when in the actual discharge of their functions. Even the costume which they wear on these occasions is not properly sacerdotal. It is only an ancient court uniform. All Shinto priests are appointed by the civil authorities. They have no 'cure of souls,' and their duties are confined to reading the litanies and seeing to the repairs of the shrine.

THE PRIESTHOOD

Priestesses.—In ancient times it was the custom to attach a virgin princess of the Imperial blood to the great shrine of Ise. All great shrines have a corps of girl dancers for the performance of the sacred pantomimes (Kagura). The latter, on reaching a marriageable age, usually resign their office, and are merged in the general population.

CHAPTER VI

WORSHIP

WITH a few exceptions, of no great importance in Shinto, the outward forms of the worship of the gods have been previously made use of as tokens of respect to living men. Whether I take off my hat to a lady or on entering a church, the act is the same, it is the ideas associated with it that make the difference. The word worship must therefore be used with caution. We ought not, for example, to assume that ancestor-worship is necessarily divine worship. It may only mean acts indicating affection and reverence for the dead, common to ourselves with non-Christian peoples, and need not involve any superstitious belief in a supernatural power exercised by dead forefathers or heroes. In modern Japan, ancestor-worship is a comparatively rational cult, and it is surely undesirable that missionaries should create for themselves great and needless difficulties by condemning it indiscriminately.

Gestures of Worship.—In Shinto, as in other religions, bowing is a common form of respect to the gods. It is the custom to bow twice before and after making an offering. Kneeling is also known, but is less usual. I have not met with any case of prostration as an act of adoration. Clapping hands was in ancient Japan a general token of respect, now confined to religious worship. Sometimes a silent hand-clapping is prescribed in the rituals. Offerings and other objects used in worship were raised to the forehead as a mark of reverence.

Offerings were in the older Shinto regarded as tokens of respect, and were not supposed to be eaten, worn, or otherwise enjoyed by the deity. There is, however, a more vulgar current of opinion according to which the god actually benefits in some obscure physical way by the offerings made to him.

The general object of making offerings is to propitiate the god or to expiate offences against him. Sometimes it is very plainly intimated that a *quid pro quo* is expected.

The original and most important form of offering was food and drink of various kinds. The cardinal feature of the great ceremony by which the Mikado inaugurated his reign was an offering of rice and sake to the Sun-goddess. Other food-offerings were cakes, fruit, vegetables, edible seaweed, salt, water, and the flesh of deer, pigs, hare, wild boar, and birds. There were no burnt-offerings or incense. Next to food, clothing took the most important place. Hemp and mulberry-bark fibre, with the stuffs woven from them, are frequently mentioned. They are now represented by the Gohei. These are wands to which scollops of paper are attached, and are to be seen in every shrine and at every Shinto ceremony. Sometimes the god is supposed to come down and take up his temporary abode in the Gohei.

Skins, mirrors, jewels, weapons, and many other articles are mentioned in the Yengishiki enumerations of offerings.

Human Sacrifice.—We nowhere hear of human sacrifices in connection with official Shinto. But there are several indications of the existence of this practice in ancient times. River-gods especially were propitiated by human victims. Human figures of wood or metal are frequently mentioned, but it is doubtful whether these were by way of substitutes for living persons.

Slaves were dedicated to some of the more important shrines. Presents of horses are often mentioned. Albinos are usually selected for this purpose. They may be seen at the present day stabled near the entrance to all the important shrines. Pictures of horses are often substituted for the animals themselves. Galleries are sometimes provided for the reception of these and other *ex voto* works of art. The carriage (mikoshi) in which the deity, or rather his *shintai*, is promenaded on the occasion of his annual festival is a very elaborate and costly vehicle. The miya or shrine may be regarded as a kind of offering. Miya means august house, and applies equally to the palace of a sovereign or prince. Originally there was no building but only a consecrated plot of ground which was deemed to be the dwelling of the deity. The miya is not a tomb. The shrines are purposely small and simple edifices. In 771 a 'greater shrine' had only eighteen feet frontage. The majority of the existing 150,000 to 200,000 shrines of Japan are tiny structures easily transportable in a cart or even a wheelbarrow. To the larger shrines are usually attached an ema-do (horse-picture hall), a small oratory for the use of the Mikado's envoy, and a stage for the Kagura, or pantomimic dance. A number of smaller shrines to other gods who are in some way associated with the chief deity may usually be seen within the precincts. The approach to a

Shinto shrine is marked by one or more honorary gateways of the special form known as tori-i, literally bird-rest, from its resemblance to a hen-roost. It has its analogues in the Indian turan and the Chinese pailoo, and is doubtless of exotic origin. It is not mentioned in the older books.

Prayer. — The *Kojiki* and *Nihongi* contain scarcely any notices of private individual prayer. But there are abundant examples in the *Yengishiki*, and other authorities, of the official liturgies known as *norito*, addressed by the Mikado, or his vicars, to various Gods or categories of Gods, on ceremonial occasions. They contain petitions for rain in time of drought, good harvests, preservation from fire, flood, and earthquake, for children, health and long life to the sovereign. Sometimes the wrath is deprecated of deities whose services had been vitiated by ritual impurity, or whose shrines had been neglected. Important national events were announced to them. There were no *norito* addressed to deceased Mikados before 850, when Jimmu Tenno was supplicated to spare the life of the reigning sovereign, who was then dangerously ill. Shinto prayers are for material blessings only.

Rank of Deities.—In the seventh century a

system of official ranks was introduced into Japan from China. It was extended from the Court functionaries to the Gods, and was very prevalent in the eighth century. A curious feature of this practice was the low rank given to the deities. It was seldom that they received so high a rank as that of a Minister of State.

Kagura.—The Kagura, or pantomimic dances with masks and music, representing some incident of the mythical narrative, has been at all times a prominent part of Shinto religious festivals, and, as in other countries, has become the parent of the secular drama.

Pilgrimages are an ancient institution in Japan. Even the Mikado paid occasional visits to the shrines in or near Kioto. At the present day most Japanese think it a duty to make a pilgrimage at least once in their lifetime to one or more of the most famous Shinto fanes, and believe that their success in life depends on their doing so. Clubs are formed for the purpose, the subscriptions going to pay the expenses of these fortunate members who are selected to represent their fellows. Pilgrim trains take the place of our excursion trains. Boys and girls frequently run away from home in order to make a pilgrimage to Ise.

CHAPTER VII

MORALITY AND PURITY

Moral Code.—Shinto has hardly anything in the shape of a code of morals. The Ohoharahi, a service in which the Mikado, by divine authority, declared to his ministers and people the absolution of their offences against the gods, makes no mention of any one of the sins of the Decalogue. M. Revon, the author of a valuable treatise on Shinto, challenges this statement, which I had already made in my *History of Japanese Literature*. He maintains that from a comparison of the Decalogue and the Ohoharahi, ' Il résulte avec évidence que tous les commandements essentiels du Décalogue (sur le meurtre, le vol, la fornication, etc., se retrouvent dans notre rituel.'[1] In view of the importance of the subject, and of M. Revon's acknowledged competence as a writer on Shinto, it is desirable to examine this assertion more closely. His ' etc.'

[1] See his *Shintoisme*, p. 15, *note*.

64

puzzles me. I am unable to find in the Ohoharahi the smallest trace of any of the seven
commandments which it covers, and can only
suppose that it is a mere flourish of M. Revon's
exuberant imagination. It will be seen that for
the 'adultery' of the Decalogue M. Revon has
substituted 'fornication.' Is it not a *cas pendable*
to tamper with the ten commandments in this
way? But neither adultery nor fornication are
mentioned in the Ohoharahi. Incest *is* included
in the latter's schedule of offences, but, *pace* M.
Revon, incest and adultery are distinct offences.
Theft is *not mentioned* in the Ohoharahi. The
planting of skewers (of offerings in rice-fields) is
one of its offences, but even if the commentator is
right who conjectures that this was done for a
dishonest purpose, I submit that so highly specific
an offence is by no means the same thing as the
far more general theft of the Decalogue. The case
of 'murder' of the Mosaic code, and 'the cutting
of living bodies' of the Ohoharahi is more com-
plicated. Murder is at the same time more and
less comprehensive than the corresponding Shinto
offence. The Jewish prohibition is more exten-
sive, as it includes murder by poison, strangling,
drowning, etc., and it is more restricted as it omits
minor injuries. But there is a profound difference

E   65

between the motives which prompted the two prohibitions. It is the crime of taking away human life which is condemned in the Decalogue: the Ohoharahi objects to wounds as nasty, unsightly things, unmeet for a God to look upon or to be in any way associated with. Self-inflicted wounds, the cutting of dead bodies, or wounds inflicted by others, caused uncleanness just as much as the wounding of others. Justifiable homicide required absolution equally with felonious murder. In a word, the Japanese offence was ritual, the Jowish moral.

There are moral elements in the Ohoharahi, but they are scanty, and M. Revon greatly overestimates their importance. Not only does it contain no explicit mention of any of the sins of the Decalogue—which is all that I contended for —but it has hardly anything which even implicitly condemns them. Shintoists do not deny this feature of their religion, but claim that the absence of a code of ethics is a proof of the superior natural goodness of the Japanese nation. It needs no such artificial aids to virtuous conduct.

Purity.—But if ethics are conspicuously absent from Shinto, the doctrine of uncleanness holds a prominent position. Actual personal dirt was obnoxious to the gods, as is evidenced by the frequent mention of bathing and putting on fresh garments before the discharge of religious functions. Sexual acts of various kinds, such as the consummation of a marriage, incest (within narrow limits), interference with virgin priestesses, menstruation and child-birth, were accompanied with disabilities for the service of the gods. Curiously enough, adultery, though cognisable by the courts of justice, did not entail religious uncleanness. Disease, especially leprosy (as in the Mosaic legislation), wounds and sores involved various degrees of pollution. The death of a relative, attendance at a funeral, touching a dead body, pronouncing or executing a capital sentence, all incapacitated a man temporarily for the discharge of religious duties. Lafcadio Hearn thought that the *miya* or shrine was a development of the *moya* or mourning house, where the dead bodies of sovereigns and nobles were deposited until their costly megalithic tombs could be got ready. This view harmonises nicely with Herbert Spencer's well-known theories, but an ancient Shintoist would have considered it not only erroneous, but blasphemous. As in ancient Greece, the gods had nothing to do with such a polluting thing as death. Shinto funerals, of which we have heard a good deal of late, were unknown in ancient Japan. They date from 1868. Shinto shrines have no cemeteries attached to them. Eating flesh was formerly not considered offensive to the gods, but later, under Buddhist influence, it fell under prohibition. The fire with which impure food was cooked also contracted impurity. To avoid the danger of such defilement, fresh fire was made by a fire-drill for all the more important ceremonies. Everything Buddhist, rites, terms, etc., were at one time placed under a Shinto tabu. When a festival was approaching, the intending participant was specially careful to avoid (*imi*) all possible sources of pollution. He shut himself up in his house, refrained from speech and noise and ate food cooked at a pure fire. A special *imi* of one month was observed by the priests before officiating at the greater festivals. An *imi-dono* (sacred hall) was a hall in which purity was observed, *imi*-axes and *imi*-mattocks were used to cut the first tree and turn the first sod when a sacred building was to be erected. If, in spite of all precaution, defilement took place, consciously or unconsciously, various expedients were resorted to for its removal. Lustration was the most common. After a funeral, it has been the rule at all periods of Japanese history for the

relatives of the deceased to purify themselves in
this way. Izanagi, after his visit to Hades,
washed in the sea. Salt is sometimes dissolved in
the water used for this purpose, and is employed
in other ways to avert evil influences. Spitting,
rinsing the mouth, and breathing on an object to
which the impurity is communicated, are familiar
practices. Human figures were sometimes breathed
upon and flung into the sea in order to carry off
pollution. In modern times a gohei is shaken
over the person to be purified.

Ceremonial is the combination for some specific
purpose of the various elements of worship described above. The great ceremony of the Shinto
religion is that known as the Ohonihe or Daijôwe,
which means 'great - food - offering.' It is the
equivalent of our coronation, and its cardinal
feature was the Mikado's offering in person to the
god or gods, represented by a cushion, the first
rice of the new harvest, and of sake brewed from
it. A modern Japanese writer says :—

'Anciently the Mikado received the auspicious
grain from the Gods of Heaven, and therewithal
nourished the people. In the Daijôwe (or Ohonihe)
the Mikado, when the grain became ripe, joined unto
him the people in sincere veneration, and, as in duty
bound, made return to the Gods of Heaven. He

69

thereafter partook of it along with the nation. Thus the people learnt that the grain which they eat is no other than the seed bestowed on them by the Gods of Heaven.'

The Ohonihe was a most elaborate and costly function. The preparations were begun months in advance. In times of scarcity, it had to be omitted as too great a burden on the nation.

The Nihiname, or new-tasting, is the annual harvest festival when the new season's rice was first tasted by the Mikado. The Ohonihe was only a more sumptuous form of it. The English counterpart of the Nihiname is Lammas, *i.e.* loaf-mass, in which bread made from the new season's wheat was used for the first time in the Holy Communion. There was, in former times, a household as well as an official celebration of this rite. Strict people will not eat the new rice until it is over.

The Toshigohi (praying for harvest) was another important ceremony of the state religion. Not only the special gods of harvest, but practically all the divinities were propitiated by offerings, and a *norito* recited in their honour, of which the following is a passage :—

'If the Sovran Gods will bestow in ears many a hand's breadth long and ears abundant the latter harvest which they will bestow, the latter harvest produced by the labour of men from whose arms the foam drips down, on whose opposing thighs the mud is gathered, I will fulfil their praises by humbly offering first fruits, of ears a thousand, of ears many a hundred, raising up the tops of the sake-jars, and setting in rows the bellies of the sake-jars, in juice and in ear will I present them, of things growing in the great moor-plain, sweet herbs and bitter herbs, of things that dwell in the blue sea-plain, the broad of fin and the narrow of fin, edible seaweed, too, from the offing and seaweed from the shore, of clothing, bright stuffs and shining stuffs, soft stuffs and coarse stuffs— with these I will fulfil your praises.'

Kiu no matsuri (praying for rain) was a service in which the gods of eighty-five shrines were asked to send rain. To some of these a black horse was offered as a suggestion that black rain-clouds would be welcome.

Ohoharahi, great purification or absolution. This is one of the most curious and interesting of the great ceremonies of the state religion. It is often called the Nakatomi no Ohoharahi, because a member of the Nakatomi priestly clan performed it on behalf of the Mikado. It was celebrated twice a year, on the last day of the sixth and of the twelfth month, with the object of purifying the ministers of state, officials, and people from their ceremonial offences committed during the

71

previous half year. It was also celebrated on occasions of national calamity, such as an outbreak of
pestilence, or the sudden death of a Mikado.
The offerings made were thrown into a river or
the sea, and were supposed, like the scapegoat of
Israel, to carry with them the sins of the people.
The offences more specifically referred to are
various mischievous interferences with agricultural operations, flaying animals alive, flaying
backwards, cutting living or dead bodies, leprosy
and other loathsome disease, incest, calamities
from the high gods and from high birds, and
killing animals by bewitchment. There were also
local and individual purifications. In the latter
case, the person to be purified had to pay the
expenses of the celebration, and so a regular
system of fines for such offences came into existence.

Ho-shidzume no matsuri, or fire-calming-cere-
mony. The object of this rite was to deprecate
the destruction of the Imperial Palace by fire.
The Urabe made fire with a fire-drill and worshipped it. The service read is anything but
reverent. The Fire-god is reminded that he is 'an
evil-hearted child' who caused his mother's death
when he came into the world, and that she had
come back from Hades purposely to provide the

means of keeping him in order. If, however, he would be on his good behaviour, he should have offerings of the various kinds specified.

Numerous other services are mentioned in the *Yengishiki*, such as the 'Luck-wishing of the Great Palace,' the *Michiahe*, which is a phallic ritual for the prevention of pestilence, a festival in honour of the Food-goddess, one in honour of the Wind-gods, etc.

Modern ceremonies.—At the present day, most of the former elaborate ritual of Shinto is neglected or shorn of its ancient magnificence. One of the most important state ceremonies which is still kept up is the *Naishidokoro*, so-called from the chamber in the palace where it is performed. It is here that the regalia are kept, consisting of a mirror which represents the Sun-goddess, a sword, and a jewel or jewels. The ceremony, which is performed by the Mikado in person, was formerly in honour of these sacred objects, but is now apparently addressed to the tablets of the Emperors from Jimmu downwards—an instance of the progressive development of ancestor-worship in Shinto. In many private dwellings there is a Kami-dana (god-shelf) where a harahi, consisting of a piece of wood from the Ise shrine, and tickets with the names of any gods whom the household

has any special reason for worshipping, are kept.
Lafcadio Hearn says that nowadays there is also
a Mitamaya (august-spirit-dwelling), which is a
model Shinto shrine placed on a shelf fixed
against the wall of some inner chamber. In this
shrine are placed thin tablets of white wood
inscribed with the names of the household dead.
Prayers are repeated and offerings made before
them every day. The annual festivals (*matsuri*)
of the Ujigami or local patron-deity are every-
where important functions. Offerings are made,
and the god, or rather his emblem, is promenaded
in a procession which reminds one of the carnivals
of Southern Europe. There are Kagura performances which go on all day and late into the night.
There are also booths for the sale of toys and
sweetmeats, wrestling, fireworks, races, conjurors
and tumblers' performances. In short, the
matsuri is not unlike an English fair. With the
pilgrimages, it does much to help to keep alive
the not very ardent flame of Shinto piety.

CHAPTER VIII

Divination.—The most ancient official method of divination was by interpreting the cracks made by fire on the shoulder-blade of a deer. This process is known in many places from Siberia to Scotland, in which latter country it is called 'reading the speal' (*épaule*). A tortoise-shell was afterwards substituted for the deer's shoulder-blade, in imitation of China. There was attached to the palace a college of diviners whose business it was to ascertain by this means whether a proposed expedition would be successful, the best site for a shrine, a tomb, or a dwelling-house, from what provinces the rice for the Ohonihe should be taken, etc. etc. With private persons, the Tsuji-ura, or cross-road divination, was a favourite method of ascertaining the future. The person who wished to consult the god went out at dusk to a cross-roads and inferred the answer to his

75

question from the chance words spoken by the first person who made his appearance. Other kinds of divination were by the sound of a boiling cauldron, or of a harp, by lots, by beans boiled in gruel, by the head of a dog or fox that had been starved to death, and by dreams and omens. Ordeal was practised by fire and boiling water.

Inspiration. — There are frequent notices of oracles in the old records. Legend has preserved an 'inspired utterance' given forth by the Goddess Uzume before the Rock-cave of Heaven to which the Sun-goddess had retired. It consists of the numerals from one to ten! The famous legendary invasion of Korea by the Empress Jingo was suggested by a deity. Oracles had generally reference to the worship of the god concerned, directing that a shrine should be built for him, or religious observances inaugurated in his honour. They were sometimes used for political purposes. There is evidence that the inspired person, generally a woman, delivered the divine message when in a hypnotic trance. This is undoubtedly the case at the present time. Mr. P. Lowell's *Occult Japan* gives a detailed description of a séance of this kind at which he was present. There are mediums in Japan as there

DIVINATION AND INSPIRATION

are nearer home, who, for a consideration, will place their customers in communication with deceased friends or relatives.

Divination and the hypnotic trance are not recognised by modern or official Shinto.

CHAPTER IX

BUDDHISM was introduced into Japan in the sixth century, but it had at first little influence on the native religion. Two centuries later a process of pacific penetration began which had some curious and important results. The missionaries of Buddhism applied to the Shinto gods a principle which had been already adopted in China. They discovered that whether Nature-gods or Man-gods they were nothing more than avatars or incarnations of the various Buddhas. The Sun-goddess, for example, was made out to be Vairochana, the Buddhist personification of essential *bodhi* (enlightenment) and absolute purity; and deified men received the Buddhist titles of *Gongen* (avatar) or *Bosatsu* (saint). Iyeyasu, the founder of the Tokugawa dynasty of Shoguns, is the Gongen-sama *par excellence.*

Ryôbu Shinto, which was in practice little more than a form of Buddhism, was the result

78

of this process. Its principal founder was the famous Kōbō Daishi. At a later time other similar schools or sects were originated which drew their inspiration from Chinese philosophy or from Buddhism. Under these influences the true Shinto was much neglected. The Mikados themselves, after a few years of reign, shaved their heads and became Buddhist monks. One of them called himself a slave of Buddha. The greater Shinto ceremonies were omitted, or worse still, were performed by Buddhist monks, who also took possession of many of the Shinto shrines and celebrated Buddhist rites there.

It should not be forgotten that the foreign religion contained valuable elements unknown to the older Shinto, and that the latter had much to gain by their absorption. The Ryōbu Shinto inculcated uprightness, purity of heart, charity to the poor, humanity, and the vanity of mere outword forms of worship; of all which there is little trace in the older cult.

Chinese Learning.—The civilisation of Japan during the Tokugawa dynasty of Shōguns (1603-1868) was modelled on Chinese originals. Its moral ideals were drawn from the writings of the ancient sages Confucius and Mencius, and the sceptical philosophy of the Sung dynasty

(960-1278). But in the eighteenth century a patriotic reaction set in, which strove to establish more purely national standards of ethics and principles of government and religion. This movement, known as the 'Revival of Pure Shinto,' was first revealed to Europeans by a paper contributed by Sir E. Satow to the *Transactions of the Asiatic Society of Japan* in 1875. The principal promoters were Motöori and his pupil Hirata, two earnest, able, and stupendously learned writers who devoted their lives to an endeavour by oral teaching and in a series of voluminous works to the dethronement of the established Chinese ethics and philosophy in favour of a Shinto purified from Buddhist and other foreign adulterations of later times. They succeeded to some extent in this object. It was no doubt partially owing to their teachings that the Mikado was restored in 1868 to his sovereign position as the descendant of the Sun-goddess, the Shinto shrines purified from Buddhist ornaments and practices, and the monks expelled from them. In reality Motöori and Hirata's movement was a retrograde one. The old Shinto, which they wished to restore, could not possibly hold its own as the national faith of a people familiar with the far higher religious and moral ideas of India and

China, not to speak of civilised Europe. Without a code of morals, or an efficient ecclesiastical organisation, with little aid from the arts of painting, sculpture, and architecture, and with a sacred literature scanty and feeble compared with those of its foreign rivals, Shinto is doomed to extinction. Whatever the religious future of Japan may be, Shinto will assuredly have little place in it. Such meat for babes is quite inadequate as the spiritual food of a nation which in these latter days has reached a full and vigorous manhood.

SELECTED WORKS BEARING ON SHINTO

1. *History of Japan*, by Engelbert Kaempfer, 1727-1728. Worthless for Shinto.
2. *Nippon Archif.*, 1897 (new edition), by P. F. von Siebold. Good when first published, but superseded by later works, in so far as Shinto is concerned.
3. *Transactions of the Asiatic Society of Japan.*
   (a) A series of papers on ' The Revival of Pure Shinto ' and 'Ancient Japanese Rituals,' by Sir Ernest Satow. 1874-81. The serious student may safely neglect all that precedes these epoch-making articles.
   (b) The *Kojiki*, translated by B. H. Chamberlain, 1883. Accurate, indispensable for myth.
   (c) *Ancient Japanese Rituals.* The *Ohoharahi*, with translation and notes by Dr. Karl Florenz, 1899. Valuable.
4. *Transactions of the Japan Society.* The *Nihongi*, translated by W. G. Aston, 1896. Similar in scope to the *Kojiki.*
5. *Japan, an Appreciation*, by Lafcadio Hearn, 1904. Sympathetic insight, admirable style, blind acceptance of H. Spencer's philosophy, imperfect knowledge. His outlook is seen at its best in the recently published *Life and Letters* (Constable, 1907).
6. *The Mikado's Empire*, by W. E. Griffis. Useful for some aspects of modern Shinto, and the Folk-lore associated with it.
7. *The Religions of Japan*, by W. E. Griffis, 1895. Shows the relations of Shinto to Buddhism and Confucianism.

82

SELECTED WORKS BEARING ON SHINTO

8. *The Development of Religion in Japan.* Lectures by G. W. Knox, 1907. Judicious and up-to-date.
9. *German Asiatic Society of Japan. Japanische Mythologie*, by Dr. Karl Florenz. 1901. A good German translation of the mythological part of the *Nihongi*, with useful notes.
10. *Japan and China*, by Captain Brinkley. 1903. Throws light on some aspects of modern Shinto.
11. *Murray's Japan*, by B. H. Chamberlain and W. B. Mason. 7 ed. 1903.
12. *Things Japanese*, by B. H. Chamberlain. 5 ed. 1905.
13. *Shinntoisme*, by M. Revon, in the *Revue de l'Histoire des Religions*, 1905-1907. Highly recommended for its up-to-date theory, and as a comprehensive collection of facts.
14. *Shinto*, by W. G. Aston, 1905. Of similar scope to the present work, but more comprehensive.
15. *Ancestor Worship and Japanese Law*, by Nobushige Hodzumi. 1901.
16. *A Fantasy of Far Japan*, by Baron Suyematsu. 1905. These two works represent the attitude of modern Japanese towards the old Shinto.
17. A *Bibliography of the Japanese Empire* (1895). Gives a classified list of books, essays, and maps in European languages relating to Japan. Tolerably comprehensive, but inaccurate.

Printed in the United States
By Bookmasters